THE WORLD'S TRANSPORT

RAIL TRAVEL

Alan Cooper

Wayland

THE WORLD'S TRANSPORT

Air Travel

Rail Travel

Road Travel

Water Travel

All words that appear in **bold** are explained in the glossary.

Editor: James Kerr
Designer: Loraine Hayes

Cover: A goods train travelling through the Rocky
Mountains, Montana, USA.

First published in 1992 by
Wayland Publishers Ltd
61 Western Road, Hove
East Sussex BN3 1JD, England

British Library Cataloguing in Publication Data

Cooper, Alan
  Rail Travel. – (World's Transport Series)
  I. Title   II. Series
  385

ISBN 0-7502-0390-0

Typeset by Dorchester Typesetting Group Ltd
Printed in Italy by G. Canale & C.S.p.A.
Bound in France by A.G.M.

CONTENTS

Passenger travel by stagecoach.

BEFORE THE RAILWAYS

Think of a time before there were aeroplanes, cars, buses or trains and when there were very few roads. It was very difficult for people to travel to other parts of the country in which they lived. They could walk, ride on horseback or travel by horse-drawn coach. These were all slow and uncomfortable.

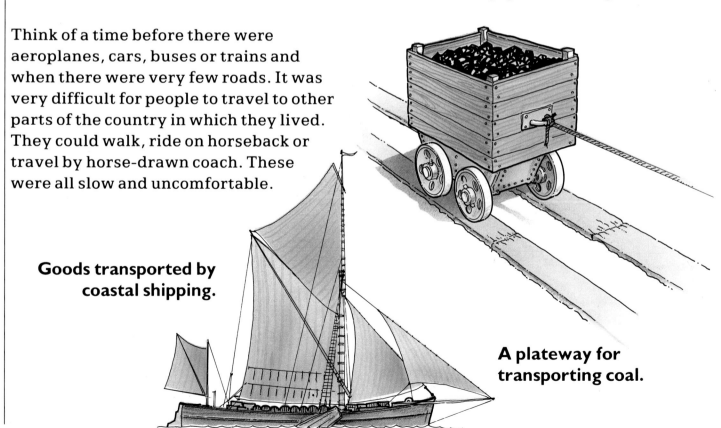

Goods transported by coastal shipping.

A plateway for transporting coal.

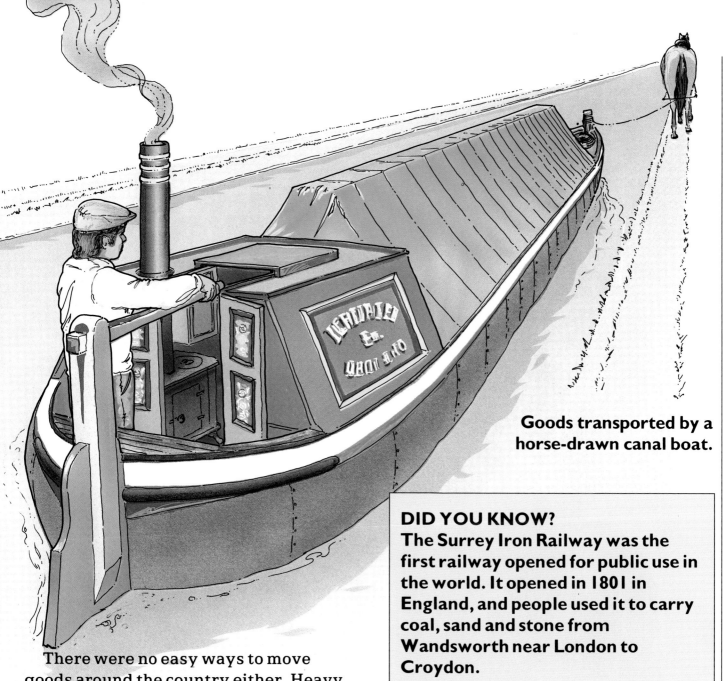

Goods transported by a
horse-drawn canal boat.

There were no easy ways to move
goods around the country either. Heavy
loads could not be carried on the roads
because road surfaces were not strong
enough. Ships could carry heavy
cargoes, but only around the coasts.
Horse-drawn canal boats could also
carry heavy cargoes, but they were
very slow.

About 200 years ago changes became
necessary. New factories were being set
up and the factory owners needed to
transport goods more quickly. In coal-
mining areas, plateways had been in use
for many years. These were flat pieces of

iron or wood laid on the ground to form a
double track. Horses were used to pull
wagons loaded with coal along the
plateways and they were very good for
carrying loads over short distances.
Slowly the tracks were improved and by
about 1800, tracks which looked
something like modern railway tracks
were being built. Horses were still used
to pull the wagons on the new railways
but they began to carry all sorts of
cargoes, and even passengers.

THE SPREAD OF STEAM RAILWAYS

Engineers in coal-mining areas tried to make steam engines that could be used on railways. Successful steam **locomotives** were made by Nicholas Cugnot in France, Richard Trevithick and Timothy Hackworth in Britain and Peter Cooper in the USA.

In the 1820s most railways still used horses to pull wagons. But in 1829 the Liverpool-Manchester Railway Company held trials at Rainhill near Liverpool to find out if steam

The Stephensons' *Rocket*, now in the Science Museum, London.

6

Celebrating the joining of the lines across the USA, 1869.

locomotives were reliable enough for regular train services. George and Robert Stephenson's *Rocket* easily passed all the tests. After 1829, steam locomotives were used on most railways.

In 1830 the Liverpool-Manchester Company ran the first regular steam-powered trains for passengers. The South Carolina Railroad began the first public steam-powered service in the USA in 1831 on a line 9.6 km long. Soon afterwards, steam locomotives began working on a 61 km line in France from St. Étienne to Lyons.

Steam-operated railways were built quickly in many parts of the world. By the 1850s steam railways were running in Australia, much of Europe, North Africa, North America and India.

Canada's first steam railway opened in 1836, and the Canadian railways are said to have 'built Canada'. The Canadian Pacific Railway, completed in 1885, linked Montreal with Vancouver, which is 4,500 km away.

The first line to cross the USA was completed in 1869. The Union Pacific Railroad began to be built westwards in 1863 and the Central Pacific was built eastwards. The two lines eventually met at a place called Promontory Point in Utah.

Early railways in Australia were built to many different **gauges**. When the Commonwealth of Australia was formed in 1901, it was agreed that a railway was needed to link the whole country. This line was built to the **standard gauge**, and opened in 1917.

A coloured light signal.

FOUR IMPORTANT INVENTIONS

The flanged wheel

Engineers had to find a way of making sure that metal wheels did not slip off metal rails. In 1789 William Jessop made wagons with **flanges** on the wheels. These guided the wheel along the rail but the wheels could run on different tracks and in either direction. Flanged wheels have been used on railways ever since.

Signalling

As more trains began to use the lines, ways were needed to let drivers know if there were other trains ahead. At first, special policemen did the job but as speeds increased, drivers needed earlier warnings. In the USA, tall poles were built with a ball that could be raised to show that a train was ahead. If the line was clear, the ball was lowered. Many other ideas were tried but eventually most countries used a system of **semaphore** arms. The position of the arm told drivers whether the line ahead was clear. At night, coloured lights were used. Today most railways use coloured light signals to show drivers if the way ahead is clear.

Westinghouse Brakes

Until the 1850s most locomotives had no brakes at all! But simple brakes were used on wagons. The **guard** applied brakes to the train but stopping was

A semaphore arm signal, still used on some slow lines.

Steam locomotives are still in use in China. The driver checks this locomotive before setting out from Harbin, Manchuria. You can clearly see the flanged wheels.

difficult. In the USA, in 1873, George Westinghouse invented brakes that could be worked from the locomotive **cab**. When the driver pulled a lever, air at high pressure forced blocks or discs against the wheels to stop them turning. These brakes were much safer and soon Westinghouse Brakes, or similar ones, were used by most railways.

Pullman Cars

Early trains got bigger, faster and safer but were not very comfortable. In 1865 George Pullman designed a new coach. It was called the Pioneer and was more roomy and comfortable than earlier coaches. It even had beds where passengers could go to sleep. Pioneers, or Pullman Cars, began to be used for long-distance travel in the USA and Canada. They were soon introduced in Britain, Europe and Australia.

A comfortable Pullman 'parlour car', built in the USA in 1876 for use by the Midland Railway in England.

HOW RAILWAYS CHANGED OUR LIVES

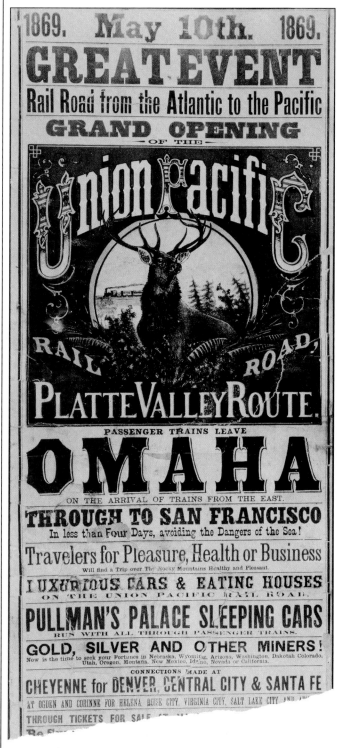

Advertising the first train to cross the USA, 1869.

Railways soon began to make great changes to life in many countries. They helped new industries to grow and helped farmers to get new machinery to their farms, or their produce to shops and markets. In the USA and Canada, railroads made it possible to farm the **prairies**. They could easily be used to carry corn from the prairies to cities or ports where it could be sent overseas. Cattle could be carried long distances by railroad and arrive at the market in good condition. The railroads ended the great 'cattle drives', when cattle had to walk hundreds of kilometres to market, driven on by cowboys.

In Britain, farmers were able to send their fresh produce to the towns every day. This improved the health of people who lived in towns. The way people spent their time began to change too. People used railways for outings. They began to see more of the country in which they lived and attractions like beach resorts became popular.

Railways even changed the time! Before railways, travel was slow so it did not matter that clocks showed different times in different places. Railways began to run services at times that were published in a **timetable**. There had to be some agreement about the times to be shown in these timetables so that everyone would know when to catch the train. In Britain, 'railway time' was introduced. This meant it was the same time in London as it was in Manchester.

RIGHT *Green Diamond*, a fast diesel-electric locomotive (USA, 1936).

LEFT 1930s streamlined express steam locomotive of the **USA**.

DID YOU KNOW?
- **In Western Australia the railway runs straight across the Nullarbor Plain for 478 km. This is the longest stretch of dead straight track in the world.**
- **The longest railway route in the world is the run of 9,438 km from Moscow to Nakhodka in Russia.**

GREAT ENGINEERING WORKS

The greatest challenge to engineers is how to carry railways across mountains or over water. Some of the greatest engineering works are found in such places.

Trains on different levels of Kicking Horse Pass, Canada.

The Seikan Tunnel
This tunnel was opened in 1987 and, at 53.85 km, it is the longest in the world. It connects the Japanese islands of Honshu and Hokkaido. Before it was built, the journey between the islands took four-and-a-half hours and storms at sea often stopped all travel. Now the journey takes fifty minutes and is not affected by storms. Cars are carried through the tunnel on special trains.

Alpine tunnels
Several tunnels run under the Alps in central Europe. The longest is the Simplon Tunnel between Switzerland and Italy, which opened in 1922. It is nearly 20 km long and made it possible for the Orient Express to travel from London to Istanbul in Turkey.

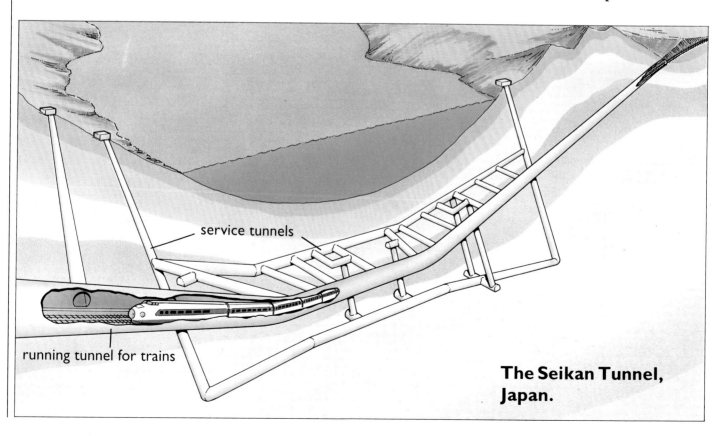

service tunnels

running tunnel for trains

The Seikan Tunnel, Japan.

The Forth Bridge

The bridge across the Firth of Forth in Scotland was opened in 1890. It is 2.5 km long and is a cantilever bridge. This means it has two great steel arms reaching out to meet each other from massive towers. The bridge is designed so that the weight of the arms is fully supported by the towers.

DID YOU KNOW?
The world's largest railway station is Grand Central Station, New York City. It covers nineteen hectares and is built on two levels. Forty-one tracks use the upper level and twenty-six tracks run underneath them. About 180,000 people and 500 trains use the station every day.

The Sydney Harbour Bridge is a massive example of a steel arch bridge. It carries roads as well as railways.

Steel arch bridges

In these bridges, the railway track is carried on a deck slung beneath the massive steel arch. Some of the best-known steel arch bridges are the Hell's Gate Bridge across New York's East River, the Sydney Harbour Bridge and the Victoria Falls Bridge linking Zambia and Zimbabwe in Africa. The Sydney Harbour Bridge carries four railway tracks as well as roads and footways. The main **span** is 502 m long and stands 51 m above the water to allow the tallest ships to pass underneath.

DIESEL LOCOMOTIVES

In Germany at the end of the nineteenth century, Rudolf Diesel tried to improve the design of engines for motor cars. In 1893 he produced the engine which became known as the 'diesel engine'.

The early diesel engines were too heavy for road vehicles but were soon used for railway locomotives and boats. By 1898, small diesel locomotives were in use in German dockyards. These diesel engines were very simple. The engine was connected to the wheels of the locomotives by a **crankshaft**. Power from the engine was transferred through the crankshaft and turned the wheels of the locomotive. Small diesel locomotives still work like this.

Diesel-electric locomotives were invented in 1924. In this type of locomotive, the diesel engine is used to produce electricity. The electricity then powers smaller motors which actually turn the wheels of the locomotive. These small electric motors are known as traction motors. A diesel-electric locomotive is really an electric locomotive that uses a diesel engine to make its own electricity as it goes along. By the 1950s, diesel-electric locomotives had replaced steam locomotives in Australia, Canada and the USA. They were also taking over from steam engines in Europe.

Diesel or diesel-electric locomotives have replaced steam locomotives because they are more **economical**. This is because they need less **maintenance** work than steam engines. They also use less fuel for each kilometre travelled, and can be driven by only one person.

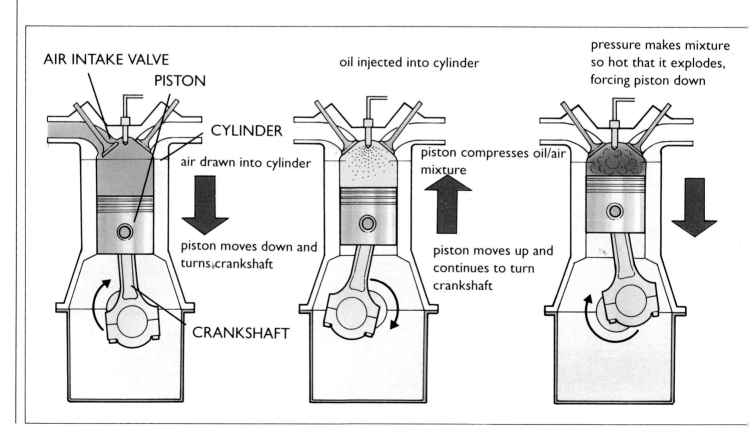

AIR INTAKE VALVE
PISTON
CYLINDER
air drawn into cylinder
piston moves down and turns crankshaft
CRANKSHAFT

oil injected into cylinder
piston compresses oil/air mixture
piston moves up and continues to turn crankshaft

pressure makes mixture so hot that it explodes, forcing piston down

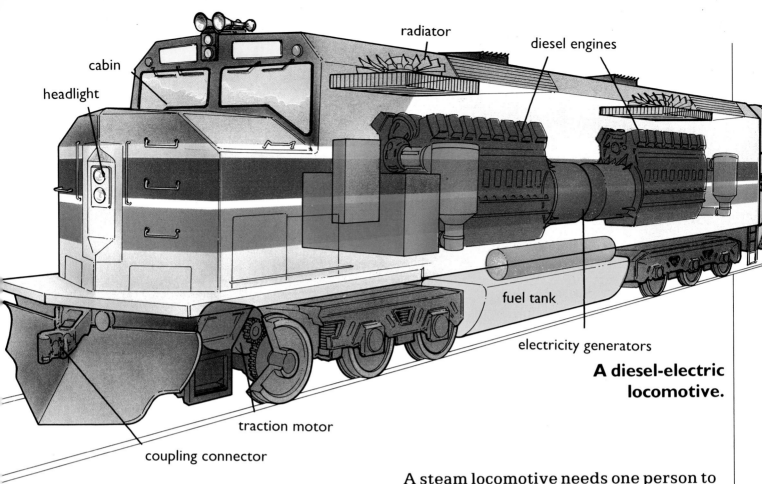

cabin

headlight

radiator

diesel engines

fuel tank

electricity generators

A diesel-electric locomotive.

traction motor

coupling connector

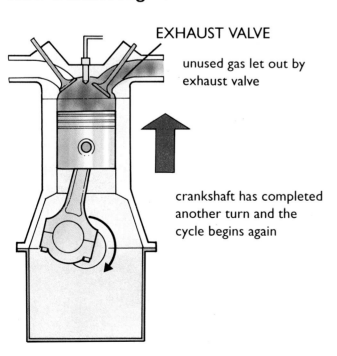

How a diesel engine works.

EXHAUST VALVE

unused gas let out by exhaust valve

crankshaft has completed another turn and the cycle begins again

A steam locomotive needs one person to drive and another to look after the fire and the water supply. With modern electrical controls, one person can drive several diesel engines hauling a heavy train.

Modern fast passenger trains and some freight trains are made up as complete train 'sets' and are rarely uncoupled except for repair or maintenance work. Some **coupling systems** are automatic. Coupling devices on the ends of the locomotives, coaches or wagons close over each other as the locomotive gently pushes them together. As the locomotive pulls back, the couplings tighten under the pressure.

Other systems use hooks and chains to couple the trains. This requires people to fasten the chains over the hooks. It can be dangerous work as the locomotive guides the coaches or wagons close enough to be hooked up or unhooked.

ELECTRIC LOCOMOTIVES

In an electric locomotive, electricity drives the motors that turn the wheels. Electric locomotives do not carry any fuel; they get their power from supplies outside the locomotive. Some use special 'shoes' under the locomotive to pick up electricity from a third rail. More commonly, the locomotive has an attachment known as a 'pantograph' which picks up electricity from overhead wires. This system is used throughout Europe and for very fast passenger services in Australia, Britain, Japan and the USA.

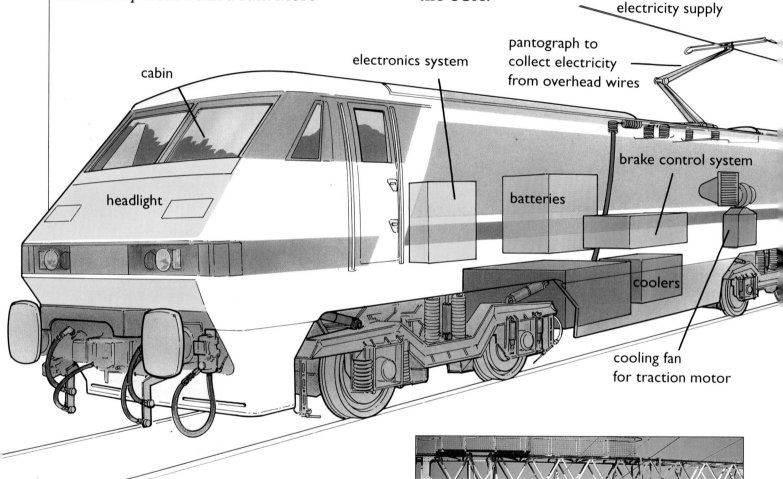

electricity supply

pantograph to collect electricity from overhead wires

electronics system

cabin

headlight

batteries

brake control system

coolers

cooling fan for traction motor

ABOVE **An electric locomotive.**

RIGHT **A British electric locomotive.**

Electric locomotives are quieter and cause less air pollution than steam or diesel locomotives. They can **accelerate** faster and travel at higher speeds. They have not taken over all the work of diesel engines because they can only operate where the special tracks or overhead wires that supply electricity have been built. This is very expensive to do, so electric trains only run where there is a lot of passenger or goods traffic.

Driving a modern locomotive

A driver's job may seem easier now than in the days of steam locomotives. The driver sits in a comfortable cab and uses a small lever to control the speed of the train. In the most modern locomotives, this lever commands a computer. The computer controls the engines and ensures that exactly the right amount of power is produced. Some locomotives are so powerful that if the power is applied too quickly, the couplings to the wagons or coaches would be torn away. Where there is no computer to help, the driver must use the power with great skill.

Drivers have to know the correct speeds for all the sections of track along which they are travelling. They must ensure that the train does not travel at an unsafe speed. They cannot fall below the required speeds for very long or the train will be running late. This delays their train and others behind it. The driver also has to watch out for signals. Drivers of fast trains on busy routes have to take note of signals and decide what action to take every two or three seconds. So modern train drivers have little time to wave to people as they pass!

The layout of a modern British train driver's cab.

UNUSUAL TRAINS

Some railways have been built to do special jobs that ordinary trains cannot do. Other special railways have been built because the engineers were trying to improve on ordinary railway designs.

Rack railways

Normal trains cannot work on steep **gradients**. To help trains on mountain tracks, a rack railway is used. This is a system where **cogwheels** on special trains fit into teeth on a special track. This gives the train more grip as it goes up or down the steep slopes.

Monorails

Some railways have only one rail and so are called monorails. These usually operate in city centres and parks. The trains may sit on the track or may be slung underneath it. The oldest monorail is at Wuppertal in Germany.

ABOVE **The rack rail system helps this train in the Alps.** RIGHT **The monorail system in Wuppertal, Germany.**

Rope railways

Before the Rainhill Trials, many people thought rope haulage was the best way of moving trains. The trains have ropes or chains attached and these are pulled by stationary steam engines. Rope railways are still used in some hilly areas.

Armoured trains

Special trains were built to carry soldiers in wartime. To protect the soldiers, the trains were fitted all round with heavy steel plate. Some trains carried huge guns to fire at enemy soldiers many kilometres away. These trains were first used in the American Civil War (1861-65). Very large guns were mounted on armoured trains in the First World War (1914-18).

A British armoured train of the First World War.

WHO USES RAILWAYS? GOODS

Railways carry heavy cargoes over long distances. Most goods are now carried by container trains. The goods are loaded into huge containers which are taken by train to a port, where the containers are loaded on to a ship. After a sea voyage, the containers are put on another train to be carried to their **destination**. This saves a lot of time and reduces damage to goods because they are only handled at the beginning and end of the journey.

Coal is carried by rail in many countries. In Britain, 'merry-go-round' trains take coal to power stations. These trains load and unload coal automatically without stopping at the colliery or at the power station.

Cars travel by rail! New cars can be carried by rail from factories to garages. Some people put their cars on special

A modern freight train on the Union Pacific Railroad, USA.

transporters if they are travelling a long distance to go on holiday. They can use their cars after the rail journey.

Special rail wagons are used to carry oil and chemicals for use in factories, and to take grain from farms to mills for making flour. A new kind of truck for use on road *and* rail has been introduced in North America and Europe. This vehicle means that goods do not have to be

A road/rail goods wagon.

A British 'merry-go-road' train carrying coal.

transferred from road to rail vehicles. In the USA, trains of more than 100 wagons, pulled by several diesel engines, can carry cargoes of 10,000 tonnes. In South Africa, a goods train weighing nearly 70,000 tonnes and over 7 km long was run in 1989. Sixteen locomotives were needed to pull the train! It was the heaviest train ever run and it travelled 861 km in two days.

WHO USES RAILWAYS? PASSENGERS

When people have to travel long distances, they usually travel by air. Many people use cars for shorter journeys. So who uses railways?

Commuters

Lots of people live many kilometres outside cities like New York, London, Paris or Tokyo but rely on transport to travel to work every day. Such people are known as 'commuters'. Some travel by car or bus, but thousands of people are carried to and from the world's great cities by rail every day.

In large cities, trains travel underground to help people move easily around the city. The first underground services were steam operated but soon they all switched to electric trains. The New York Subway, the Paris Metro, the London Underground and the Moscow Underground are famous examples of railways built underground to make city travel easier.

The Japanese *Shinkansen*.

DID YOU KNOW?
The busiest railway in the world is the East Japan Railway which carries 14,666,000 people every day.

A modern tram car in Italy.

Trams

Trams are light railways that run on narrow-gauge track laid along city streets. Horse-drawn trams were used in the nineteenth century to help people to move around large cities. All modern trams are powered by electricity which they take from overhead wires. They are linked to the wires by a long pole which has electrical connectors. The electricity powers motors that drive the wheels of the vehicle. Trams have driving cabs at both ends of the vehicle, so there is no need for them to be turned round when they reach the end of a line. Amsterdam in The Netherlands is well known for its tram cars. Many large towns have a tram system.

Holiday travel

Many people use trains to get to their holiday destinations. In Canada, *The Canadian* express runs through the Rocky Mountains during the summer as a tourist attraction. Some famous expresses in the USA, such as the *California Zephyr* and the *Empire Builder,* also run mainly for people on holiday. Faster and more comfortable trains have encouraged more people to use trains for holidays in Europe too.

The French TGV *Atlantique* on its record breaking run, 1990.

DID YOU KNOW?
The French railways run the fastest trains in the world. The TGV ('*Train à Grand Vitesse*' or 'high-speed train') holds the world speed record for any train. On a special run, a TGV travelled at 515 kph. In regular service, the TGV *Atlantique* is designed to run at speeds up to 300 kph.

TRAIN TECHNOLOGY

Railways make use of the most up-to-date equipment so that trains can run safely and provide better services.

Better signalling is needed as trains run faster. By using computers, long stretches of track and many trains can be controlled by one person. The trains show up as coloured lights on a huge electronic board so that the controller can tell the exact whereabouts of any train. The controller then directs the trains to ensure that they all run safely.

Drivers are warned by a flashing light and a buzzer or bell if they pass a yellow 'caution' signal. They must press a button to show that they have seen the signal. If they do not do so, the brakes come on automatically. There are automatic devices to stop trains passing signals showing red for 'danger ahead'.

The fastest passenger trains, like the Japanese *Shinkansen* and the French TGV *Atlantique,* run on what is called 'dedicated track'. This means that no other trains can run on these tracks, so the trains can maintain very high speeds. The tracks for the TGV *Atlantique* have very few signals. This is

A railway station as seen on a computerized signal system screen.

because the trains travel so fast that drivers could not see signals in time to take action. All information about the track ahead and what the driver needs to do, is sent to computers on board the train. These computers then show the information to the driver on a screen in the driving cab.

Computers also provide information for passengers. They help passengers to plan their journeys. New trains in Germany have computer services for business travellers and videos for passengers who do not have work to do!

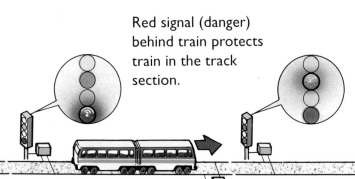

Red signal (danger) behind train protects train in the track section.

Signal green because no train in section. Next signal will be green or double-yellow (preliminary caution).

Electrical system detects train on track.

Signal green because no train in section. Next signal green or double-yellow.

ABOVE Like the French TGV, this Japanese *Shinkansen* uses special tracks.

How a modern signalling system works.

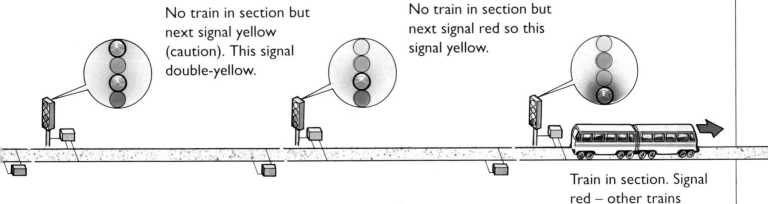

No train in section but next signal yellow (caution). This signal double-yellow.

No train in section but next signal red so this signal yellow.

Train in section. Signal red – other trains must stop.

WHAT WENT WRONG?

Not all the work of railway engineers has been successful. At high speeds, trains lean over as they go round bends and passengers feel uncomfortable. In the 1970s, British engineers designed a train with a tilt system. As the train went round bends at high speed, it would lean over but the passengers would be kept level. The experimental trains travelled round bends successfully, but when passengers used the trains, the tilt system made them feel sick!

Modern technology cannot prevent all accidents or delays to trains. Most accidents are caused by a breakdown in signalling, so that drivers do not know that there is a problem ahead of them. Modern trains have good brakes, but they are so fast and heavy that they can take two kilometres or more to stop if they are travelling at high speed. So even if drivers see danger ahead, they cannot always avoid it.

Trains can be delayed for many reasons. The track may be blocked by a

The experimental British 'Advanced Passenger Train' speeding round a curve.

Disasters can occur even on modern railways. This accident happened when signals failed to work properly at Clapham, near London.

broken-down train or snow. High winds can damage the wires carrying the electric current to electric trains. When this happens, the trains cannot operate at all.

All railway services work hard to prevent delays but they cannot always be avoided. Where trains run on dedicated track, there should be fewer delays for passengers. In Japan, passengers can claim refunds of part of their fare if the trains are seriously delayed.

Snow has been cleared away for this German express.

DID YOU KNOW?
The worst ever railway disaster happened in France in 1917. Eight hundred people were killed when the brakes failed on an over-loaded train.

RAILWAYS TODAY – AND TOMORROW

A driverless MagLev train at Birmingham International Airport, England.

In the 1950s, railways all over the world lost traffic to road services and to air transport. For long distances, aeroplanes are much faster than railways, so passengers used the new air services.

Railways cannot carry goods all the way from a factory to a customer because railway lines do not go to every factory or every house. Passengers have to travel to a station to board a train. Because lorries and cars can transport passengers and goods to an exact destination, traffic moved on to roads.

In the 1980s passengers and goods began to move back on to the railways.

There are so many road vehicles that road travel has become slow and unpleasant. Trains are getting faster and more comfortable and they can carry much heavier loads than road vehicles. In the USA, even long-distance trains are carrying more passengers.

People are becoming worried about air pollution caused by road vehicles. Electric trains cause little pollution, so countries like France, Germany and Italy are developing new railway services to try and encourage rail transport. New road/rail vehicles are being used to carry goods direct from factories to customers.

The tunnel which runs under the English Channel, connecting Britain with the rest of Europe, is known as the Channel Tunnel. It is designed for railways only. Special trains have been developed to carry road vehicles. These trains have been built with two decks to carry cars and lorries. They have passenger lounges so that people making the journey across the Channel can travel in comfort. Passengers can expect to travel from Folkestone to Coquelles near Calais in France in thirty-five minutes. Up to seven trains per hour should run in each direction every day.

Construction works for the Channel Tunnel, linking England and France by rail.

The new Channel Tunnel express trains will be even faster than present ones but perhaps travel by ordinary railways cannot get very much faster. At Birmingham and Stansted Airports in Britain, MagLev trains run without wheels or rails and have no drivers! They run by 'magnetic levitation' which means they are lifted by powerful magnets. The magnets lift the train so that it hovers just above the track, and special electric motors move the train along. The trains' movements are controlled by computers from a central control office. In the USA and Japan, MagLev trains have been run in tests at over 300 kph. In the next hundred years, our modern trains will seem as odd as the early steam-engines seem to us.

GLOSSARY

Accelerate To increase speed.

Cab The driver's compartment.

Cargoes Large loads of goods.

Cogwheels Wheels with teeth which fit into holes in a chain to obtain a better grip (you can see these on bicycle chain wheels).

Coupling systems Ways of connecting trains together.

Crankshaft A metal arm which transfers the up and down movement of a piston in the cylinder of an engine to wheels, making them turn.

Destination The end of a journey.

Economical Not wasteful; cheap to operate.

Flanges Projecting rims on one side of a wheel on a railway vehicle.

Gauges The distance between the rails of a railway track.

Gradients Upward or downward slopes.

Guard The official in charge of a train.

Locomotives Railway engines that are mounted on wheels and can move under their own power. They pull coaches and wagons.

Maintenance Keeping a machine in good working condition.

Prairies The large grassy plains of North America.

Semaphore A code using an upright post with arms which can move up or down to give information to drivers.

Span The distance between the ends of a bridge.

Standard gauge A railway track with a distance of 56.5 inches (1.45 m) between the rails; used on most railways.

Timetable A printed list showing times at which trains (or other vehicles) will arrive at, or depart from, a particular place.

BOOKS TO READ

A Day in the Life of British Rail Edited by Murray Brown (David and Charles, 1989)
Modern Locomotives by Brian Hollingsworth and Arthur Cook (Salamander, 1983)
Railways by David Roberts (Kingfisher, 1992)
Steam Locomotives of the World by Colin Garratt (Ladybird, 1979)
Train Technology by Michael Pollard (Wayland, 1989)

Trains by David Jefferis (Franklin Watts, 1991)
Trains by Jonathan Rutland (Usborne, 1991)
Transport by Eryl Davies (Franklin Watts, 1992)
Transport by Robin Kerrod (Wayland, 1991)

Picture acknowledgements

The publisher would like to thank the following for providing the pictures used in this book: ET Archive 6, 7, 9 (bottom), 11 (left and right), 18 (bottom); Eye Ubiquitous cover, 8 (bottom), 9 (top), 12, 16, 19, 20, 21; Colin Garratt 24; Topham 10, 13, 23 (right), 26; Wayland Picture Library 8 (top), 17, 22, 23 (left).

The artwork is provided by Nick Hawken.

The author wishes to thank the following for their help in compiling this book: British Rail Research, London Road, Derby (Miss S. M. Jones); The French Embassy; French Railways; The Japanese Information Centre, Grosvenor Street, London.

INDEX

The numbers that appear in **bold** refer to captions.